Briar Creek – A Visic

Briar Creek – A Vision of Faith

Copyright 2010

Dedication:

I want to dedicate this book to my best friend, my wife Gretchen. Without her at my side, this vision would only be half complete. She has stood by me during our hardest times when my faith was being tested. I look forward to seeing what plans God has for us in the years to come.

I love you,
Mike

I also want to give a special thank you to Kay Young. She has been my editor and encourager through the whole process. Gretchen and I look up to you and Abe as our adoptive parents. We just hope we can stay as strong in the Lord as you both have been.

"Now faith is the substance of things hoped for, the evidence of things not seen. For by it the elders obtained a good testimony. By faith we understand that the worlds were framed by the word of God, so that the things which are seen were not made of things which are visible." Hebrews 11:1-3

Dear Father,

As I share this vision, may it bring glory to You alone. May it inspire, cause others to pray, and possibly invigorate a communication with them and Your Holy Spirit so they can have a hope in something unseen in their lives. May we come to the realization that all our thoughts and ideas come from You and, like a mustard seed, sometimes our ideas just need a little soil to help them to grow. Please show us how to plant Your ideas so they produce fruit that is acceptable and stamped with Your approval. I pray this prayer in the name of the Lord of my life, Jesus Christ.

Amen

Chapter 1 - The Vision

In the fall of 2005, while worshiping in my church on the island of Guam, the Lord gave me a vision. It was not, and has never been, an out-of-body nor seen-by-my-eyes type of vision. Instead, pictures of unknown things and ideas I could never come up with fill my mind. Each time a vision has been given to me, it has always been during a time of worship to the Lord and always when I have prayed for the Holy Spirit to come upon me.

The vision He first revealed to me has constantly evolved. Little by little the Lord has shown me more pieces to the puzzle as He prepares me on this journey. Like Moses at the burning bush, the Lord only shows us those things we are capable of comprehending at the time. How much faith is needed if God reveals all things at once?

The initial vision was this: "I want you to build a retreat center for pastors and their families. I want it located in Theodosia, Missouri; and I want you to build your house and on it put the name "Faith" because this place will be built upon it. Then I want seven cabins for the pastors and each will be given a name representing a fruit of the Spirit: Love, Joy, Peace, Patience, Kindness, Goodness, and Gentleness. I want you to put "Self Control" on your garage to remind you not to fill it with a bunch of toys."

I know the scriptures say that God is no respecter of persons, but during His speaking I sensed His deep love for pastors and that, as a church, we have neglected many of them. I especially felt that the ones neglected the most were younger ones, missionaries, youth pastors, and worship leaders.

I said to the Lord, "Lord, if you want me to be a pastor, just tell me and I'll do it. But, I feel unqualified to minister to pastors who would come to the retreat center." The Lord said, "That isn't what I want you to do; I just want you to love them where they are...I will do the ministering."

Then the Lord revealed that I was to construct a path, a trail through the woods. He showed me that I was to name it, "The Names of God Trail," and He revealed different things He wanted built on the walk to represent some of His names. I know there are many names of God, but the ones He initially wanted on the trail are:

* Jehovah - Rohi (The Lord, My Shepherd)
* Jehovah - Jireh (The Lord shall Provide)
* Jehovah - Shalom (The Lord our Peace)
* Jehovah - Rapha (The Lord our Healer)
* Jehovah - Tsidkenu (God of Righteousness)
* Jehovah - Makkah (God Who Smites)
* Jehovah - Gmolah (God of Recompense)
* Jehovah - Shammah (God of Presence)
* Jehovah - M'Kaddesh (God Who Sanctifies)
* Elohim Sabaoth - (God of Hosts)

One of the last things initially revealed was the name of the place. I didn't know why at the time, but the Lord gave me the name "Briar Creek" for the name of the retreat center.

Now that you know the vision, it's time to back track and how you the Lord's hand in this for over 30 years.

Chapter 2 - First Act of Faith

At the beginning of fifth grade, my doctor discovered that I was near-sighted. I could read anything directly in front of me, but after about ten feet it was blurry. He prescribed glasses to bring my vision back to 20/20. Initially, wearing glasses didn't seem too bad. They were stylish wire rims and I can't recall being made fun of by any of my classmates.

That all changed prior to seventh grade. The wire rim glasses got broken and my parents didn't have the money to replace them with the same style. The lenses were still good but I had to find a frame that would, 1) fit my existing lenses, and, 2) be cheap enough to afford. The only frames that fit the bill were black plastic. I didn't care for them but made the best of it. Of course, my classmates in junior high quickly gave me the nickname, "mad scientist."

Those years were hard on me but not so much due to the glasses. I was finding myself more a loner than ever. Friends weren't always acting like friends unless it was convenient for them. I had several cousins living nearby and usually I found myself hanging out with them, even though most of the time I felt they were being nice to me because they had to.

The main reason for setting myself apart at my Catholic grade school was to discover who I was spiritually. Thanks to my parents having an open mind and for an awesome teacher, a nun named Sister Sharon, I was exposed to the Charismatic Catholic movement in the late 1970s. It was during this time that I originally asked Jesus to enter into my heart and life. I discovered some of the priests were Spirit-filled, although they seemed to be rare exceptions. I considered the priesthood for my own life, and if it wasn't for some solid advice from my Spirit-filled nun, I might have pursued it more.

During my eighth grade year Ralph, my older brother, went into the Air Force. I always admired my big brother and everything he would send home from the Air Force was just the coolest stuff. I was doing pretty well in school and I gravitated to the thought of being a pilot, a dream I had had most of my life. My brother sent me a brochure on the Air Force Academy. The thought of going there and flying for the Air Force was the dream of all dreams. What seemed to be a great idea was soon dashed by a prerequisite for a pilot. At that time, all pilots had to have 20/20 vision, uncorrected. My glasses were now an obstacle.

In June of 1979, my family was invited to attend a healing revival that was coming to the Peoria, Illinois, area where we lived. The evangelists were Charles and Frances Hunter. All week we attended the revival, and this was the first time I was exposed to so much of God's power and

His Holy Spirit. I witnessed speaking in tongues, interpretations, words of knowledge, and healing for the first time. It took me all week to drum up enough courage to ask for healing for myself.

On the last night of the revival I met Charles Hunter in the foyer and asked him if he could heal my eyes. He said, "I can't, but Jesus can." With that he laid his thumbs over my eyes and prayed for healing. After he prayed I could see that nothing had changed in my vision. But I thought to myself, "I just need to have faith." So I immediately began telling everyone that my eyes were healed.

Those around me praised God for my healing and I never put my glasses back on. I went through a week or two of headaches from my eyes, but never told anyone. It was summer time so there was no school work to do or any chalkboard to be read, so I was able to keep it going.

In mid-August, about two months after my "healing," I was walking up the alley behind my house and everything changed! The alley went up the hill to a big church parking lot. On the other side of the parking lot was a grove of tall trees. That afternoon, walking up the alley, I had been looking down at the ground and then looked up. All of a sudden the distant trees became clear. It was as if a squeegee wiped a car window glass and it just became clear. I knew at that moment faith had caused my healing.

I never did go into the Air Force or become a pilot. I did, however, go into the Navy and into the submarine service. A few years ago, stationed aboard the USS Henry M. Jackson, I had the job of periscope operator. It was my responsibility to find navigation markers and distant contacts (other ships) we needed to avoid. Every time I would see a contact before the Officer of the Deck on the other periscope, I would give God the glory for healing my eyes. Now, in my mid-40s, my latest eye exam still confirmed better than 20/20 vision. Praise the Lord!

Chapter 3 - Charismatic Catholic

I know many of you who read the title of this chapter may wince or, at a minimum, feel uncomfortable with the very thought of it. But I would be negligent not to mention this part of my life. Had I not traveled this path in young adulthood, I would not be as open to God's direction as I am today.

In this time of my life God was a loving Father, but I also saw Him as limiting my freedom. I felt the desire to please Him, but then I wanted Him to let me have fun in my youth. I became involved in the Catholic Church program called Teens Encounter Christ or TEC for short.

TEC was sponsored by the Catholic diocese to bring teenagers into a meaningful relationship with Christ. It consisted of a staff of adult clergy and lay leaders as well as some teen staff members who had already been in the program. The staff would meet for a number of weeks to go over the different talks that would be given during the weekend TEC retreat. The retreats were usually a mystery to the teens coming. What they would discover was a Saturday-morning-to-Monday afternoon of talks, projects, and events that would guide a teen to a commitment to Christ. To this day, I have not found an equivalent Protestant teen program that has the intensity and adult commitment of the TEC program.

I was privileged to be a part of five TEC weekends, counting my initial one. I took with me, when I joined the Navy right after my fifth TEC, a love for Jesus, a desire to follow Him, and a love for the community of the Church. It was during that final TEC that I asked the Lord for a sign whether or not I should join the Navy, because I was scared to leave home. Immediately after my prayer the song "Be Not Afraid" was played during the Mass. I knew that was my answer.

Chapter 4 - Recommitment in Italy

One of the challenges to today's Catholic, especially one who exposes himself to other denominations, is that there are plenty of people who want to tell you how deceived you are and how misguided your doctrine is. My view at the time was that I didn't give much credit to someone's religion if they had to tear mine down in order to build theirs up.

I did have some questions about the church stance on certain issues, namely prayers to saints, including Mary, the celibacy of the priesthood, the exclusion of women in the pastoral role, and more that are not relevant to this testimony. Though I no longer associate my calling with the Catholic Church, I still feel a deep love for it and its community.

I believe there are Catholics on their way to heaven and some on their way to hell. There is not one denomination, Catholic or Protestant, who can claim to be any different when it comes to being saved. Each church has its good and its bad, and maybe this is why I have such a love for pastors among us that put up with all types.

The next big step in my life after joining the Navy was finding my lovely wife, Gretchen, from Seattle. As a newly married couple, we noticed right away that there was something missing in our spiritual walk. We married in the

Catholic Church, attended Mass, but there was more to a walk with God and we both knew it. Still not knowing where to turn, I received orders to Italy. At first we considered this as our opportunity to get closer to our religion by being in Italy, nearer to Rome and more traditional than the American Catholic Church. We waited with anticipation for our new journey.

Within six months before transferring, our world was rocked. Gretchen learned that she was pregnant and subsequently learned she had only one functioning kidney. Most likely she was born with the condition, but it had never come up until she was pregnant.

The two of us were excited at the thought of a baby and our first child had a normal heartbeat at 16 weeks. When we went to the next ultrasound on week 20, we learned our first little boy, who we had affectionately named Tattie, had not made it. We both ached inside, but I know Gretchen hurt a lot more than I did. She had an attachment to him that I wouldn't have had until after the birth. We tried comforting each other in the fact that these things are common and God had other plans for him.

As we came closer to transferring, I learned that my father Ralph Sr. had had a heart attack back in Illinois. As my family came together to see him through, the thought of losing my dad at that point in my life was unbearable. He was my strength and

I wanted the opportunity to prove myself. I hadn't yet had the chance to make him proud. I remember praying to God, "Father, if you bring my dad through this, I will recommit my life to you." I really didn't know what it meant at the time. I later learned God is not only honored in our prayers, He often honors us in them, too, by helping the prayer along when we don't even know what we're asking.

During my return trip to Peoria I learned that Mom and Dad had left the Catholic Church; they were attending Glad Tidings Assembly of God in East Peoria, Illinois. In reality, it didn't seem too surprising. Mom and Dad were going through the same feelings of wanting more of God, and they enjoyed the worship and power of God they were exposed to in their new church. Gretchen and I visited Glad Tidings and, though we felt awkward with some things, I remember going to the altar again on behalf of my dad.

One significant event took place at Glad Tidings when we attended a mid-week Bible study. A woman prayed over Gretchen and I and she began to give a word of knowledge from the Holy Spirit that we have never forgotten. She prophesied that we were called to serve the Lord in a powerful way, but only as a team would we be successful. She told Gretchen that it may sometimes seem that I would be on a higher spiritual plane, but she was just as significant for this ministry to work. One without the other, there would be no ministry. I have since learned that Gretchen has gifts that I lack, such as discernment. Over the years I have learned to trust her feelings just as she has learned to trust when God speaks to me.

My father made it through surgery and came out in better shape than he had been in years. Gretchen and I flew off to our new home in Italy.

As we were trying to adjust to our new culture and getting to know new Italian friends, we quickly realized that our hope of getting closer to God in the Catholic Church in Italy was not going to happen. We attended Mass with four or five other American families in a small community center, but there was nothing there of any substance. Gretchen and I were on our own; if we were going to get closer to God, it was going to have to be revealed by Him. That is exactly what happened.

One morning on the ride aboard a small boat I traveled on to get to work every day, a guy was reading a book I had seen at a Christian bookstore before going overseas. I sat down next to him and asked if it was a good book. He said it was, and then asked me if I was a Christian. No one had ever asked me that question before so it sounded strange. I replied, "Well, yes, I'm a Catholic." He smiled, and eventually invited us to a mid-week Bible study.

We were excited to meet new people and so became the token Catholics at this Protestant Bible study. There was something I learned from my new friend, Don--the love of a brother. Even though we came from distinctly different backgrounds (even my Bible was different), he loved me where I was, without condemning. He just encouraged me to read the Bible more and more. He seemed to know all along that it was only God's Word that would bring me where I wanted and needed to go.

After about six months of reading my Bible and being a part of this Bible study and community of believers, I felt the Lord speaking to me for the first time. I felt Him leading me out of the Catholic Church. He was showing me that the traditions and doctrines that I thought so important were no more important than what the Pharisees thought important in Jesus' day. He was telling me that all He wanted was to have a relationship with me.

As the Lord continued to speak to me in His Word, Gretchen and I made the decision to no longer identify ourselves as Catholics, but instead as just Christians. It was more difficult than one can imagine. It was like taking a brick wall and dismantling it brick by brick. At first there was a lot of guilt, but it turned into real freedom in the Lord.

Let me say at this point to my Catholic friends, this is what the Lord called me to do. Each person must "work out your own salvation with fear and trembling, for it is God who works in you both to will and to do for His good pleasure"

(Philippians 2:12b-13). I would be out of line to ever expect my journey to be the way for all. If the Lord has placed you in the Catholic Church and that is where your conscience rests easy, then that is where you need to be. All who are saved through Jesus Christ are part of His body.

> "For as the body is one and has many members, but all the members of that one body, being many, are one body, so also is Christ. For by one Spirit we were all baptized into one body - whether Jews or Greeks, whether slaves or free - and have all been made to drink into one Spirit. For in fact the body is not one member but many." (1 Corinthians 12-14)

For my Protestant brothers trying to talk to your Catholic brother, I exhort you to do it in love. If love isn't your motivator, nothing will be heard.

That summer, Gretchen and I decided to be baptized as adults since we had previously been baptized as infants. Don baptized the two of us on a Mediterranean beach near Palau, Sardinia.

Chapter 5 - Angel in Naples

We learned that with Gretchen's kidney condition, she would always be considered high risk during pregnancy; and also she would not have the care she needed if she got pregnant again because of where we were going in Italy. We were told during our overseas screening process that if she got pregnant in Italy, the Navy would be forced to bring her back to a stateside hospital to deliver the baby.

We were using the natural family planning method of birth control approved by the Catholic Church. We were having success with it, but seven months after moving to Sardinia, Gretchen found out she was pregnant. I guess God had plans for a baby in our lives and didn't want us to wait. As promised, the Navy carried through with sending my wife back to the states. At the time I was underway on my ship to the Italian seaport of Gaeta.

Gaeta is a small port about halfway between Rome and Naples. As the ship was pulling into Gaeta, I received word that Gretchen was being medevaced (medical evacuation) to the hospital in Naples. She was to undergo some tests for about four days and provided everything looked good, they would medevac her to the states from there.

I went into severe depression, looking at the prospect of being separated for at least ten months. She was already one-to-two months along and would not be able to fly back to Sardinia until the baby was two months old. My thoughts that September were that I would miss Christmas with Gretchen and the spring birth of my first child.

Another thought going through my mind was how to be able to afford this. You have to realize that there weren't any storage facilities in Sardinia. I couldn't just pack up our apartment, put it in storage and live on the ship until Gretchen and the baby returned. I needed to keep the apartment so she and the baby would have a home to return to. I also needed to supply enough money for Gretchen to live on in the states. You can imagine the frustration and despair I was feeling. I was numb and in shock.

The ship pulled into Gaeta and I was informed to take the train down to Naples as they were going to let me off for the four days in order to say good-bye to Gretchen. I got off the ship and proceeded to find my way to a city I had never visited. I knew that bus tickets in Italy are bought in Tabacchi (or Tobacco) shops and I saw one after leaving the gate of the port. I went in, bought a ticket, and went across the street to the bus stop.

The only prayer I remember praying that morning on my way to Naples was asking that the Lord help me get to Gretchen. The bus showed up right away, which didn't surprise me at the time, but I later learned this bus only ran about every hour-and-a-half. The bus took me the ten miles to the train station. Walking into the first train station in my life, I saw on the big board the next train to Napoli (Naples) and what track it would be on. I bought a ticket and proceeded to the track. Once I got there, the train showed up right away. This train had a 30-40 minute schedule, another "coincidence." On the train there was one event that I would later feel was significant.

I should tell you at this point that, as American service members, it was our goal to try to blend into the civilian population while overseas. We were instructed to try not to bring attention to ourselves in our actions or with our clothes. By the time I made this journey, I tried to dress and look Italian as much as possible. I must have been successful in this attempt because half-way through my hour-and-a-half-long trip down to Naples, a group of Italian teenagers were taking pictures of each other and at one point asked me (in Italian) if I could take their picture (at least that's what I think they asked). When I opened my mouth, they realized I was not Italian, said, "Ahh, Americano," and then left me alone.

Upon reaching the train station in Naples, I got off my train onto the large platform between two tracks. There were at least 20 tracks that converged together, and at the end of each platform was a huge terminal building. I saw the building ahead of me and the thought of being lost was not in my mind. Little did I know that as soon as I walked in those doors, I would find out real fast that this place was not as easy to manipulate as an airport, especially to a non-Italian-speaking American. I might have assumed there would be some type of USO or other American military information counter, but either way, I was not yet in the building so I wasn't lost "yet."

Out of the blue, an Italian-looking, middle-aged man grabbed my arm and said in perfect English, "Go through these doors and take the escalator downstairs. Catch the train to Pozzuoli. Get off at Campi Flegrei and find bus 26, it will take you were you need to go."

I was shocked by the abrupt nature of his stopping me and after he said his instructions, all I could say was, "Thanks." I started to walk away and then thought I should tip him, so stopped and turned back around to give him some money. He had vanished! In my state of mind, the thought of having an angel guiding me took a few days to sink in.

I did what he had instructed me and when I got down the escalator, the Pozzuoli subway was just pulling up. After boarding the train, I saw that the Campi Flegrei station was six or seven stops away. When I arrived at Campi Flegrei and walked out of the train station, there must have been 25-to-30 orange busses lined up. I finally found No. 26 and even though the doors were open, the bus was not running and there was no driver. As soon as I entered the rear of the bus and had my ticket punched by the machine, the driver came from out of nowhere, started it up, and we were on our way.

I must have been on the bus for a good 20 minutes when I noticed a large fence and an area that looked like a military base. Inside the fence was a Wendy's restaurant and I knew we were at the Naval Station. I rang the bell and as I was exiting the bus, out the front window saw a young woman in bright pink shorts crossing the street toward the American Hotel. It was Gretchen! The Lord had brought me right to her with the help of one of His messengers and in record time.

On subsequent visits to Naples over the next few years, I would sometimes be given the job of duty driver. Never, in my future trips from Gaeta to the Naval Base in Naples, was I able to beat the record time of that first trip.

Chapter 6 - All Alone

After spending those four days in Naples with Gretchen while she was being readied for her trip back to the states, I didn't know how I was going to make it through the next nine-to-ten months. She was about two months into her pregnancy and the baby was due in April. We knew that the baby would have to be at least two months old before she could return to our home in Italy, so it was going to be a long separation.

Returning to our home in Sardinia was very painful. My focus became how I could make it to the states to see Gretchen and how I could be there for the birth. During the pregnancy Gretchen was going to live with her mom and dad, so my thoughts were constantly of how I could get to their home in Seattle for Christmas. An opportunity presented itself that could save me a lot of money.

Around Thanksgiving the USS Gato, a submarine based out of Groton, Connecticut, pulled up next to my ship, USS Orion. I was down on the submarine making some repairs to their photo-copying machines when I learned that one of their crew members needed to go home on emergency leave. This was going to strain the crew on their return transit because this crew member was one of their Quartermasters (they determine the submarines position on a chart and help to navigate the boat). I volunteered to get underway with them since I was a qualified quartermaster, and could still be fixing their copiers on the way back to Connecticut. Also, I told them of my situation and that I needed a cheap way back to the states. A plane ticket from Connecticut to Seattle was a lot cheaper than one from Sardinia.

The USS Gato was due to pull into Groton the week before Christmas so the plan seemed like a great opportunity. The submarine Captain liked the idea and asked my skipper if I could go. My Captain refused, and that was upsetting. It was hard to trust God during that time because it seemed I just could never get a break.

A week or so later, the home fellowship I had been attending asked me to come up front of the congregation on Sunday morning. They, along with a dozen or so other families, had taken a special collection and raised enough money to make the plane ticket within reach. It was a humbling experience to have others care this much about me. I learned a lot about how we love one another and how vital it is in our Christian walk. I also learned that God truly does have good things in store for us, because I later found out that the USS Gato got extended out at sea and did not pull back into their homeport in Groton until after the New Year. If my skipper had allowed me to ride back with them, I would have definitely missed Christmas with Gretchen.

When it came time for our first child to be born, the doctors decided they would induce the birth early due to the stress on Gretchen's one kidney. This also meant I would know when the baby would be born. During this time my ship did me another favor. They sent me to Groton, Connecticut for a Navy school during the early part of March and this allowed me to be in Seattle when my first son, Michael, was born on March 27, 1992.

One mystery we had during Michael's birth was that during the 66 hours of labor, there was a nurse named Maggie who seemed to show up when Gretchen needed the most encouragement. When the decision was made to do a C-section, I took our video camera into the delivery room. On the tape, we can clearly hear Maggie talk and when Michael was pulled from the womb, we heard Maggie say, "There's our little bumpkin."

The mystery, however, is that after Gretchen and Michael went back to her mom and dad's home and later came back for a visit with the nurses prior to returning to Italy, she asked them where Maggie was. The nurses said there was never a Maggie that worked there. When Gretchen showed them her pictures, each nurse said she had never seen her before.

A few months after Michael was born, Gretchen and Michael were back on a plane to Olbia, Sardinia, and we were together again.

Chapter 7 - Finding a Church

One thing Gretchen and I had never needed to worry about was where we were going to go to church. When we moved back to the states after those four years in Italy, we were not going back as Catholics. Previously our church would have been the nearest Catholic Church, but now we didn't know where we would end up. One thing I had hoped to find was a church that had a Wednesday night service. I was so hungry for the Lord; I really wanted a mid-week service to supplement the normal Sunday service.

We returned to the state of Washington and one of our friends we knew from Italy invited us to his church. The worship was good and the message was on the mark, but there just seemed to be something lacking in the body. We had previously agreed that we would visit each church at least twice, so we planned to return the next Sunday. The down-side of this church for me was there was no mid-week service. Since they didn't have one, I felt it wouldn't hurt if we tried another church out on Wednesday night.

The next Wednesday night we visited Olympic View Assembly of God in Silverdale, Washington. We sat in the back and before the service started the pastor came up and introduced himself to us. His name was Larry Reed. Both my wife and I discerned right away that this was where God wanted us.

Under the guidance of Pastor Reed I learned more about being a Christian than at any other time in my life. Those years at Olympic View molded me into being a true disciple of Jesus Christ. I learned the power of prayer and saw the awesome power of the Holy Spirit. It was also during this time that our marriage went through its greatest test.

In a period of five years, we lost four more children. In each case, Gretchen was forced to carry the child for a long period of time before the doctors decided it had to come out with a D&C. Each loss grieved us and strained our relationship. We finally came to the conclusion that Michael would be our only child and guessed that was what God had planned.

Though we struggled during those years, one of the greatest demonstrations of what faith can do was also realized.

Chapter 8 - Faith Groceries

In the summer of 1999, I was underway on a submarine, my good Christian friend with me. I was discussing with Rob how I wanted to exercise my faith when we pulled back in. My idea was to pick some Saturday and go somewhere to pray. We would ask the Lord to show us what groceries we needed to buy. Then we would pray for Him to show us the place to deliver it. I told him I just wanted to see what the Lord would do.

He agreed to go with me, so we picked a Saturday in July and after meeting for breakfast, found a park and sat at a picnic table to pray. I had a notebook and Rob said he would pray first while I wrote down what the Lord would show me. Immediately after Rob started praying, several brands of products started flooding my brain. I wasn't receiving words like "cereal", but specific products like "Life" and "Cheerios". As I wrote "Cat chow," I felt the Lord tell me, "You will find two cats on the porch." As I wrote cake mix, ice cream, and frosting, I was told, "There will be a celebration in this house soon." Throughout the list the number seven was to play some significance. By the time Rob was done praying, the shopping list was complete, so we went shopping.

When we exited the store, we were in a pretty nice part of town, near the base. I told Rob it didn't matter, I wanted to take it where the Lord led us; I didn't want to be influenced by any human emotion to take it to a poor neighborhood.

We started driving around the town and I looked for cats...but didn't see any. After about ten minutes, Rob pulled over so we could pray some more. After praying, he asked me where I thought we should go. I was reluctant to tell him because the place in my mind was a poor neighborhood. He told me to tell him anyway, so I told him I saw this mobile home park on the other side of town. He agreed and that's where we headed.

When we arrived, we saw the mobile home park was a big circle and it had one drive down the middle. We drove the entire perimeter first, and as we did, I again looked for cats...again, not any.

As soon as we turned into the center drive, the first mobile home had one cat on the porch, so Rob stopped. The address was 28, and even though I didn't know what the "seven" was for, I thought it might be part of the address. Besides, there was supposed to be two cats, not one. We continued on.

When we got to the second-to-last mobile home, there were two cats on the porch. The unit didn't have a number on it, but the one next to it was 72, so it seemed maybe this was 70. Besides, it did have two cats. We were starting to feel uncomfortable as we drove into the driveway. There wasn't a car in the drive, so it looked like no one was home. We got out of Rob's car and felt like maybe we should pray some more. Just then this young lady opened up the door while holding a little girl was in her arms. She asked us if she could help us, and Rob said, "Ma'am, this may seem strange to you, but my name is Rob Crouch and I go to Peninsula Bible Fellowship, and this is Mike Hatcher and he goes to Olympic View Assembly of God. We were out praying today and felt the Lord lead us to your home to drop off these groceries. We aren't trying to get you to come to our church or anything, but just want to know if you would be willing to accept them without any obligation." She immediately started crying and said she would love to have them.

We started carrying in the groceries and she turned to me and asked me where it was again I went to church. I told her and she said, "Maybe you know my mom; she goes there." I asked her name and when she said her mom's name, I was blown away. I said, "Of course, I know your mom." You see, her mom had come to church by herself for years and whenever the Pastor asked for prayer requests, she would always lift up her daughter and husband who were not saved.

Here I was in the living room of a person I had prayed for many times. The other amazing thing was, not only were we going to witness the events of this day, I was going to be able to find out what happens after we leave, because I know her mother.

This really gave my faith a boost, so I then asked her, "Could you tell me if there is going to be a celebration in this house in the next few weeks?" She said her daughter, Chelsea, would be turning two next week. I told her she would find a cake mix, frosting, and ice cream in the bags. She really started crying then. Anyway, we left her house and I was excited to see her mother the next morning at church.

When we arrived at church, her mother came running up to me right away. What I learned was that this young woman's mother and father had been helping her and her husband through a difficult time. That Friday night, the father told his wife to stop giving help to their daughter. Her mother told the daughter she couldn't go against her dad, so she could no longer help them with money. On Saturday the daughter told her mother, "This morning, I prayed to God that if He was real, He would provide for us. Then these two guys came by bringing me seven bags of groceries."

It was then I realized what the seven was for; it hadn't occurred to me there were seven bags. She told her mom all these products names as she was unloading the bags saying things like, "Chelsea's favorite cereal," and her husband's brand of shaving cream and shavers, etc.

Eventually, this simple act of faith brought a young mother and her husband to church and a recommitment to the Lord.

Chapter 9 - Submarine Life

I continued going out to sea with a rotation of three months out and three months in port. This time was very hard on Gretchen and Michael. I hated being away from them and Gretchen started to develop signs of depression, which made it even harder. During those few years, even though I desperately wanted to get closer to my wife, she seemed more distant. I also wanted to get closer to God, but it seemed like He had forgotten about me. Every time we got underway, I felt like I was heading off to serve a prison sentence.

As my relationship with Gretchen suffered, we both were trying to fill the empty void in our lives. We decided to have a foreign exchange student for different school years. We took a girl from Italy and then a boy from Finland. These relationships gave Gretchen and Michael something to fill their void; I filled mine with pornography.

I became addicted to pornography, which was easy to do on a submarine of 180-or-so men. Inside, it was eating me alive. I was trying to live a Christian witness, but felt the guilt and shame for what was going on in private. I questioned my salvation and was constantly asking the Lord for forgiveness. I prayed that all I could do was trust that He would somehow rescue me from my addiction.

On returning from sea, I tried a number of things to keep from succumbing to the temptation on the internet. Thinking if I just stayed busy there wouldn't be enough time to get into trouble, I volunteered for anything I could do at the church. Another solution was to never be home alone. When Gretchen was home, I was less likely to surf the wrong websites.

Another painful consequence was that I felt I couldn't share my failures with my Christian brothers. Having experienced the outcome of confession before, I was afraid to make the same mistake. It was okay to admit you were a sinner and that you depended on God's daily dose of grace, but if you admitted to a previous addiction (pornography or any other vice, like drugs or alcohol), other Christians seemed quick to conclude you lacked the ability to serve the church in any capacity. You were tainted and made to feel like a second-class Christian.

The problem with an addiction is that you may get through a period of time, like two-to-three months, without falling into the sin and you begin to feel you have finally been delivered. Then you let down your guard and, usually out of the blue, find you are right back into the thick of it; you have once again opened the door.

Because I didn't feel it was possible to share what I was dealing with, I felt even more alone. My mind became so twisted that I even started blaming my addiction on my wife. I had thoughts about leaving her, but thankfully, the Holy Spirit showed me that I wouldn't be able to get through it without her help.

During this dark night of my soul I found myself in, there were still times when God would allow me to witness His favor. One such event came as my submarine was just getting underway and a piece of my equipment failed. After troubleshooting the unit, my technical manual stated that the fault was one of three circuit cards. The next step in the procedure was to replace the A2 card, A3 card, and then A7 card. Each time a card was replaced, the unit was to be checked to see if the faulty symptom went away. As soon as it went away, you would know which card was bad. The problem was none of these three circuit cards was onboard the submarine.

After a week of being underway, our submarine would briefly return from sea and conduct a personnel transfer near Port Angeles, Washington. Not only would a tug boat come out to take off a few of our riders, it was also a chance to get a mail bag, some fresh milk, and any parts we may need. I promptly requested to order all three circuit cards so I could continue the troubleshooting. My skipper was a harsh man and most of the crew was afraid of him. He told me to figure out which circuit card I would need because he was not going to allow me to order all three. I thought, "What am I going to do?"

I went into the Navigation Center where I worked and started pleading for guidance from the Lord. I prayed He would show me which circuit card was the one needed. I closed my eyes and rested my head on the chart table. When I opened my eyes, the chart on the table had 7s written all over it. I took it as a sign to order the A7 circuit card, so I did.

We pulled into the Straits of Juan de Fuca and did our personnel transfer. I got my new part and plugged it in. It was the right one, praise the Lord! Just as I was buttoning up the unit, the Captain came into the control room and saw that the equipment was up and running again. He asked me, in the presence of a number of people, how I knew which card to order. I said, "Sir, it may be hard to believe, but I prayed that God would show me what part to order and I felt He told me the A7 card, so that's why I ordered that one." He stood there dumbfounded, mumbled something under his breath, and walked away. I wondered if he would take my beliefs out on me, but he didn't. As a matter of fact, he seemed to leave me alone after that.

During Sunday mornings underway, I would attend church services. We didn't have any Chaplains underway, so we had a volunteer who felt led to conduct the services. I volunteered to teach the Protestant service in the Wardroom, where the officers eat their meals, and other guys would conduct the Catholic service and a Mormon service in other parts of the ship. One thing I started doing during that time was something I continued to do on every submarine after that. When the service was over and everyone had left except my close friend Rob, we would lay our hands on the chairs, starting with the Captain's. We prayed for the Lord to help the men and give them the wisdom and knowledge they needed to do a good job. I noticed that when we started doing this, not only was the crew less uptight, but also, during inspections, we started doing very well as a boat.

Chapter 10 - Becoming a Baptist

For a number of years, Gretchen participated in a women's group called Bible Study Fellowship. She went to this non-denominational group once a week and then had homework that proved to be pretty challenging. She told me she hoped I could one day attend the men's BSF meeting that was held on Monday nights. I promised that as soon as I got off the submarine and was working in port on shore duty, I would join them. That finally came in the summer of 2000. The men happened to meet at Sylvan Way Baptist Church, and I'll never forget that first night.

When I walked into the sanctuary, I felt this overwhelming peace come over me. When I got home, I told Gretchen about it and that I wasn't sure if it was the guys at BSF or the church. I asked her if she would be willing to go with me to Sylvan Way the next Sunday and she agreed.

We visited the church the following Sunday and she confirmed the feeling of peace that I felt. When asking the Lord what it meant, I felt the Lord telling me to move to this church for a season. At first it didn't seem to make any sense. Here I was, a speaking-in-tongues-Pentecostal in the middle of a Baptist church and I had no idea how they would accept me. We did admit to the pastor during our membership orientation that we were going to be speaking-in-tongues Baptists and he just said, with pure kindness, "Praise the Lord!"

It didn't take long to figure out why God had moved us to this church. What I found in this Baptist church was a love for God's Word. Even though the Assemblies of God loved God's Word too, they emphasized the power of the Holy Spirit more. Whether they realized it or not, the diligent seeking of God's power affected the emphasis that was placed on the Word.

What I noticed was a constant craving for the supernatural and the "feelings" received from the move of the Holy Spirit. I don't want to diminish those experiences, but there must be time given to the priority of studying scripture. The love of study was in this Baptist church. Though there were plenty of Baptists who feared or discredited the move of the Holy Spirit with signs and wonders, they did give me a renewed attitude for the Word.

For two years we stayed at Sylvan Way and this was when I had the breakthrough I longed for.

But first, the dream...

Chapter 11 - The Dream

One night I had a dream. In it, I was standing on the back deck of a house with a group of people I didn't know. It was twilight and the deck of the house overlooked a marshy field. Suddenly, from behind the house, just over where I could see the gutters against the roof, there was a huge fireball zooming through the sky. The meteorite was traveling quickly across the sky and it was so big that if it were to hit the earth, it would cause devastating damage. However, in my spirit, as I watched it go from one end of the sky to the other, I didn't feel any fear or panic that it was going to strike the earth. Instead, all around me, the crowd of people who were with me said in unison, "It's Psalm 19, it's Psalm 19." At this point, I woke up.

Unlike most times when I wake from a dream and remain half asleep, this time I completely woke up. Not knowing what was in Psalm 19; I quickly opened my Bible and looked it up. I read,

"The heavens declare the glory of God; and the firmament shows His handiwork. Day unto day utters speech, and night unto night reveals knowledge. There is no speech nor language where their voice is not heard. Their line has gone out

through all the earth and their words
to the end of the world. In them He
has set a tabernacle for the sun,
which is like a bridegroom coming
out of his chamber, and rejoices like
a strong man to run its race. Its rising
is from one end of heaven, and its
circuit to the other end; and there is
nothing hidden from its heat."
(Psalm 19:1-6)

I marveled at the awesomeness of God
using a dream to display His Word. I didn't think
anything more about the dreams significance until
over a year later.

During our two years at Sylvan Way, I
attended their annual men's retreats. I don't recall
the specific lessons that were talked about, but
there was a deep concern I had and privately I went
to the Lord about it. I still struggled with my flesh,
specifically the internet pornography. It was getting
close to time to return to submarine duty and I
knew that as soon as I got back on that boat, the
temptation would return and didn't know what to
do about it. I was having relative success in
resisting the temptation, but knew that I probably
would not be able to resist the level of pornography
I would be exposed to on the sub.

I remember praying to the Lord to rescue
me from the "miry clay." At the first retreat, I

talked to the youth pastor and for some reason told him about my Psalm 19 dream. He said I ought to return to Psalm 19 because there might be more the Lord was trying to tell me. I took his advice and I remember that night as I read the last half of Psalm 19:

> "The law of the LORD is perfect, converting the soul; The testimony of the LORD is sure, making wise the simple; The statutes of the LORD are right, rejoicing the heart; The commandment of the LORD is pure, enlightening the eyes; The fear of the LORD is clean, enduring forever; The judgments of the LORD are true and righteous altogether. More to be desired are they than gold, Yea, than much fine gold; Sweeter also than honey and the honeycomb. Moreover by them your servant is warned, and in keeping them there is great reward. Who can understand his errors? Cleanse me from secret faults. Keep back your servant also from presumptuous sins; Let them not have dominion over me. Then I shall be blameless, and I shall be innocent of great transgression. Let the words of my mouth and the meditation of my heart be acceptable in your sight,

O LORD, my strength and my
Redeemer." (Psalm 19:7-14)

It cut me like a knife. I knew what I did in
private, knew my secret faults. Right then, I
experienced what it means to have a contrite heart.
I had finally come to the point of knowing I
couldn't get through this addiction on my own. I
said something like, "Lord, I can't do it. If you
don't renew my mind, I will fail. You are the only
one who can do it." There was nothing I could
personally do with this struggle except turn it over
to Jesus and trust Him to take it away.

Then the change I had waited for happened.
My mind became renewed. Pornography no longer
gave me the same thrill or satisfaction. After this,
when encountering pornography, I starting seeing
the women in the pictures as victims. The pictures
would give me the same feeling that a crime photo
would. Jesus had rescued me and I knew it. My
flesh sometimes desires the return to my old self,
but I have the ability to resist by coming to Jesus
each time.

By the time of my second men's retreat, a
year later, I was asked to teach the men about
overcoming the flesh. As soon as that retreat was
over, I knew the Lord was about to move us again
because I felt closure to that season.

It was also during that season another
miracle took place in our family. By this time, we

had Michael, who was eight years old, we had lost five children and the emotional roller coaster was taking its toll on us. Just as we were coming to the realization that we were only going to have one child, Gretchen came up pregnant for the seventh time. At first we thought, "Here we go again," but we really wanted to believe that God would grant us this child. We made it through the first heartbeat test and then the second, but there seemed to be a problem in the ultrasounds. They discovered the baby would be a boy and we named him Aaron.

The ultrasounds showed Aaron to have extra thick skin on the back of his neck and his umbilical cord only had one artery and one vein instead of the normal two arteries, one vein cord. These two things made it very likely that he would have Down syndrome. We were counseled that having an amniocentesis would better determine the fact and the military doctor we were seeing was telling us, without ever saying it, that he thought we should abort the baby.

We immediately told him that we had no intention of going through an amniocentesis and that this baby would go full term. He tried to persuade us that if we knew for sure, it would give us more time to prepare. It didn't matter what he wanted us to do, we were not going to subject the baby to it. Our feeling was that if God gave us a child with Down syndrome, it would tell us His Will in full color.

Many people pray all of their life to know what God's Will is or what purpose God has for them. Our feeling was that if this child had a special need like Down syndrome, we would never have to question our purpose again. We would have this child and he would be our purpose.

When Gretchen had one of her early ultrasounds, she told me about one ultrasound technician. After seeing what it looked like on the screen and it showing the possibility of Downs, the technician asked Gretchen if she could pray for the baby. The technician laid her hands on Gretchen's tummy and prayed for a healthy child. Our church prayed for Aaron as well.

On May 14, 2001, Aaron was ready to come out. We got to the hospital and after the operating room was ready, he was born. He turned out to be a healthy boy. We know that God has placed a special hand on him. To this day, he has said he wants to someday be a pastor. He has, on numerous occasions, laid hands on those who are sick and they have been healed. I pray God continues to move in his life.

It was time for me to return to submarine duty and so our family moved to Indian Island, Washington.

Chapter 12 - Indian Island

I returned to submarine duty aboard the USS Henry M. Jackson. For the next two years I discovered a place of peace, a place of goodness, and a lot of it had to do with joining the Irondale Evangelical Free Church. I was out to sea for Thanksgiving and Gretchen had attended a church service near our new home that was being celebrated by the area's local pastors (seven in all). She wrote me an email saying she sensed the Holy Spirit really working in the life of the pastor from the Free Evangelical Church. His name was Pastor Dave. She asked me if we could go there for a visit once I returned...of course I agreed.

The genuineness of its members drew me to the church. I sensed a lot of caring for each other. We had just left the Baptist church that was so large it was easy to just go with the flow and never really get involved. In Irondale they needed help from every member. Because the whole church was involved, none of it became a burden or ever felt like it could burn me out.

It was at Irondale that Gretchen and I were able to do something we had never had the chance to do before--lead an adult marriage class. It wasn't anything spectacular, but it was the first time that our ministry worked together. It was during this time I saw a glimpse of how we were supposed to minister from that time forward; it really made ministry fun.

The downside of living so far away from everyone on our little island (there were 14 families on the whole island), was that when we went to sea Gretchen had her most difficult times with depression. My time away was taking a toll on her and I knew something was going to have to give.

My time on the Jackson was very rewarding. The Captain was a born-again Christian and I was part of a Chief's Quarters where I loved every one of the guys. The Lord had really blessed me to be part of that team. It was no surprise that this same crew would win the "best crew" award for the squadron.

A very influential event took place after I returned from a Christmas patrol at sea. We had left around Halloween and missed Thanksgiving and Christmas again. We were due to return in early January, so before we left Gretchen and I had agreed we would buy our Christmas gifts for one another when I returned and we would celebrate Christmas a few weeks late.

On Christmas morning, Gretchen and the two boys, who were about twelve and three, had Christmas alone. When I returned home, my 12-year-old told me about their Christmas morning. "Mom had only one gift under the tree", he said. My oldest sister had sent her a tin of specialty popcorn. My son said it was a sad morning because he could see in his mother's eyes that she felt all alone...she felt abandoned. She just wished the day would go by quickly.

Upon returning from sea and hearing his account, I realized this would be my last submarine. My family was saying, without saying it verbally, "Dad, we've had enough!"

There was another important lesson the Lord needed to teach me about faith and it happened when we got back from sea. It had been at least four years since we delivered groceries by faith in the mobile home park. Out of the blue, the Lord stirred me to do it again. This time He said, "Take $200.00 out of the ATM, go to the Safeway in Port Townsend and go to the third register from the door. You will find a lady wearing red. Pay for her groceries and just tell her, "God loves you." This seemed easy enough and I was excited to do it. As a matter of fact, I couldn't rest until it was done.

The next Saturday I planned to drive into Port Townsend, but we also had another event where the family had to be. I told Gretchen I just needed a few minutes to go and do this thing and we ended up getting into a big argument. Eventually I was just frustrated and wanted it to be over with. We drove up to Port Townsend and instead of going to the ATM; I figured it would save some time to just go in and pay for the groceries with my debit card.

Going into Safeway, I saw an older lady parked in a handicapped spot putting her groceries into her trunk. She was wearing red. I walked by her and entered the store. The third register from the door was just closing. I stood there and asked the Lord, "What happened; how did I miss it?" He told me in a very stern voice, "You were not obedient."

He reminded me that I was instructed to pull the money out of the ATM. This wasn't so much a mission to tell a woman that God loved her as it was a mission to learn to follow God's instructions to the letter. He reminded me that Moses had been told to speak to the rock in order to get water, but in his frustration struck the rock instead (Numbers 20:11). For Moses' disobedience he was not going to be able to lead his people into the Promised Land (Numbers 20:12). I was deeply hurt for my disobedience and I vowed never to do it "my" way again.

Even though my orders were for me to be on the Jackson for two more years, the submarine was going into the yards for repairs, so it was necessary to downsize the crew. I saw this as an opportunity to take my family to our next adventure, and that turned out being in Guam.

Chapter 13 – Guam

My detailer (the guy who tells me where I am going to go and for how long), released me from my obligation on the Jackson because I was willing to move to Guam for two years on the USS Frank Cable. We really loved Guam because we had so much family time. Even though Guam is an island, we had a lot to do because we loved being together. Between the days at the beach or trying out a new culture, we found our niche in a non-denominational church that had a good mix of locals and military members.

I enjoyed the church because there was some solid Bible teaching, but there was something building inside of me that I couldn't immediately put my finger on. After about a year on Guam, we decided that I would ask to stay there for another year, making our total time there three years instead of two. The biggest benefit was that since my next shore duty would be for three years following Guam, if we allowed our oldest son to do his freshman year at Guam High, he would be able to graduate just when I would be retiring.

One day as I sat with a few of the men at my church, I shared the story of "faith groceries." One of my friends, Robin, said, "I wish I could do something like that." Immediately, the Lord told me, "Do it with him, to build up his faith." I told Robin that we were going to do it. I felt the Lord prompt me to ask Robin to come up with a grocery list. I really didn't know what most Chamorran's ate. I asked Robin to come up with a two-week supply of food and stay away from refrigerated or bread products. Waiting for Robin to come up with the list, I prayed God would show me where to take the groceries. The Lord showed me the statue of a Chamorran Chief Gadao in the village of Inarajan, Gaum, on the southern end of the island. He told me to go down the road that is across the street from the statue and that a dog would lead the way.

On the following Sunday, Robin had his list ready. We agreed to split up the list and buy the groceries that week. We also agreed we would deliver them the following Saturday. As the week went by we got our groceries and, since it was all non-perishable, they could just be kept in the trunks of our cars.

As Saturday drew closer, so did a typhoon. By the time Saturday arrived, the whole island of Guam was in a category-one lockdown, so we were all stuck in our homes. If that wasn't enough to deter us, I came down with a high fever and became almost paralyzed in bed. As the typhoon got closer and closer and just before it reached us, it shifted and went north. When the storm passed, so did my fever.

We were fortunate that the following Monday was a holiday and we were both off of work. We got together and drove down to Inarajan.

When we got to the statue of the Chief, we noticed
there were actually two roads that were about equal
distance and perpendicular to the statue. Since we
had already passed one of the roads by the time we
got to the statue we went down the next one. It was
a one way street and people were everywhere,
looking at us with a look that told me we were not
welcome. There were also dogs everywhere so I
knew we needed to go around and get to the other
road.

When we turned down the right road there
were no people and as soon as I followed the street
around a corner, a dog was sitting in the middle of
the road. The house behind the dog had a big
"Beware of Dog" sign in the window. I knew this
was the house, if you could call it a house. None of
the windows had glass, just blankets covering the
holes. The house was made out of cinder blocks
and it appeared to look more like a garage than a
home. The yard was strewn with several old
vehicles and weeds were growing around and even
inside them. The place really looked abandoned,
but we could hear dogs barking inside. We went
up to the door and knocked. After knocking three
times Robin said, "Maybe it was another house
down the street."

Just then the door opened up and a woman
asked us what we needed. I told her, "Ma'am, my
name is Mike and this is my friend Robin. We
were praying and felt that God wanted us to deliver

groceries to this home. We aren't trying to get you to go to our church, just wanting to know if you would be willing to accept them with no obligation." At this, the woman said, "How did you know?" Robin quickly responded, "We didn't!" She went on, "How did you know that my brother was sick and we didn't have any money to buy food?" I told her that God really loved her. Of all the homes on Guam, He had picked her home to have us deliver these groceries.

We carried them inside and immediately realized why they needed to be non-perishable. There was no refrigerator and I wasn't sure if they had running water or electricity. We prayed for her and her brother and then left. I don't know what the Lord did later for this family but I do know that on that day the Lord increased Robin's measure of faith a hundred fold.

. . .

In the fall of 2005, the Lord gave me the vision of Briar Creek. During the worship time at our church, the Lord showed me "Faith" and the other seven cabins with the trail. Slowly, as it sunk in, our whole lives started to shift.

Chapter 14 - Becoming a Lutheran

After receiving the vision of Briar Creek, I found myself in quite a quandary. I was attending a church that I really loved for its teaching, but it was also made very clear that the senior leadership in the church did not believe certain spiritual gifts were still functioning in the modern church era. We were being taught that certain gifts of the Holy Spirit, such as tongues, were only used in the early church. Yet, I knew and practiced this gift during my private prayer time. Here I had had a word of knowledge with the vision, but I didn't feel I had the liberty to talk to anyone in church leadership about it.

I knew my days were numbered with staying at the church, but didn't want to leave until the Lord released me. I wanted to be 100% in His will, so I was not prepared to move my family somewhere else until He told us to go.

In the meantime, Gretchen had opened up a franchise business in Guam called Kindermusik. She called it Island Kids and we had a small studio in the town of Agat, Guam. She had several kids, ranging from newborn to seven years of age, coming to the studio every week and we were enjoying relative success in the military community.

One of the projects she worked on was bringing her Kindermusik curriculum to some of the area day care centers. One day care that picked it up was the Tender Shepherd Day Care that was being run out of the Lutheran Church of Guam (LCG). Her interaction with the Lutheran Church allowed her to become acquainted with their pastor, Jeff Johnson. Pastor Jeff's demeanor impressed me when I first met him, and our family took a liking to him right away.

This became very apparent when our oldest son Michael was going through a pretty rough time. The issue he was dealing with was something Gretchen and I felt could use some pastoral counseling. We asked Michael if he wanted to talk to our current pastor. He told us he would prefer to speak to Pastor Jeff. After his one time visit with Pastor Jeff, the struggle he had been dealing with seemed a lot less important. I attributed this to Pastor Jeff's calming demeanor.

I went to the Lord and basically asked Him, "Lord, my son is afraid to go to his own pastor, do you want me to go to the Lutheran Church?" I felt Him tell me to stay at our current church. This went on for a couple of months and then my ship got underway.

While underway, my friend Bill, who attended LCG, told me he had received an email saying that the Sunday after we were due to arrive back home, Pastor Jeff would be giving a sermon on homosexuality. He had planned to announce that if the Lutheran Church of America were to approve homosexuality as a legitimate lifestyle, he would be leaving the Lutheran Church. I emailed Gretchen about it and asked her if she thought we should visit LCG in order to show Pastor Jeff our support and she agreed.

The ship pulled back in and we went to LCG that Sunday. I really enjoyed our first visit. The body of believers was very loving and we felt like we belonged right away. We found out that Pastor Jeff had already given his sermon on homosexuality and learned that the church body was very favorable with his stance on the issue.

Again, I asked the Lord if He would allow us to change churches and again He said no. A few days later, Bill told me that LCG was discussing the possibility of going independent from the Lutheran Church of America. This would take them out of the mission status and allow them to keep or hire their own pastor. The downside was they would no longer receive the financial support from the main organization. The minute Bill told me about this decision; the Lord interrupted my conversation and said very plainly, "It's time!" I knew then to move our family to LCG.

Later, at a church meeting, LCG members were discussing their independence. Half of the church was leaning toward it favorably but the other half had doubts they could afford it. I stood up and said, "I want everyone to know that I have been praying for God to allow my family to come here and join this church. It was only after I heard you were discussing the possibility of going independent that the Lord told me it was time to move here. I want you all to know that you need to trust God to provide for us because He is behind this."

We went through the membership class and quickly got involved in our new church. One Sunday, Pastor Jeff was teaching a sermon on the parable of the talents in Matthew 25:13-30 and he had the collection plate passed around. However, there was already money in the plate. He instructed us to take ten dollars out of the plate for each member of the family. He then said that in a month he would open up the floor to the congregation to give a testimony of how they used the money. Some members didn't want to take the money but we were excited with the challenge.

Knowing how God had worked before with Faith Groceries (this is the name we started calling it); we decided to use it in a similar way. We felt led to take our portion and use it as seed money to have a garage sale. We planned a garage sale and made $264.00 a few weeks later. I prayed for the Lord to show us what to do with it and He immediately showed me a small grocery store about two miles south of LCG. He told me to go into the store on the second day of the month at two o'clock in the afternoon and give the person at the checkout stand the money.

This time I wrote a letter to the person who would be getting the money. It basically explained that our church had been learning a lesson on the talents and that this money was to sow a seed into this person's life. It said, "I don't know if you are a man or woman, whether you are in need or not, but I was instructed to give this to you on this day, December 2, 2006 at exactly two o'clock." Gretchen put the money and the letter in an envelope and then we waited for the next weekend. Saturday, December 2 arrived and we got to the store about 15 minutes early.

When we went in, there were three shoppers and I meandered around to see if one of them might be the one at the counter at two o'clock sharp. By the time it was a minute or so before two, the store was empty. Then right at two o'clock, a woman with three little kids walked in. We went up to her in the aisle and told her we were instructed to give this money to her at this time on this date. I don't know what ever became of the woman, but I hope to find out someday. It wouldn't surprise me to learn that the amount of $264.00 had a direct meaning to her so she would know it was from God.

Around that same time, the Lord showed me something that He had been working on in me for the last 15 years. As you now know, I had gone from being Catholic, to Assembly of God, to Baptist, to Evangelical Free, to Non-denominational, to now a Lutheran. The Lord showed me my past and revealed that He needed me to go through these different denominations in order to break down the stereotypes I had built up against other denominations. He showed me that all of my past pastors had struggled with the same types of issues. It was at this point I realized the real meaning of what He said early on, which was to love each pastor where they are, because He would do the ministering.

Chapter 15 - Summer 2007

As the summer of 2007 came, Pastor Jeff had to return to the states to take care of some personal and church business. He brought in an intern who was studying to become a pastor. She was Pastor Linda, her husband's name was Mal, and they were from Australia. That summer was full of excitement as we were due to return to the states in September and I would be going to shore duty to retire.

Since my orders had me transferring in September, there wouldn't be much time to get moved into our new place and get the kids in school. There was definitely no time to visit my family until later. We planned to visit my father at his new home in Arkansas for Thanksgiving.

During that summer the Lord really began to move on our behalf. The first thing He did was reveal to me the significance of each pastor He had placed in my path. He showed me the name of each pastor and how the name on the cabins represented their ministries. Pastor Larry Reed: (Patience) Pastor Ric Glomstad: (Kindness) Pastor David Hodgin: (Goodness) Pastor Linda Hamill: (Peace) and Pastor Jeff Johnson: (Gentleness). Love and Joy were yet to be named, but it didn't take long.

Before returning to the states, I got word that one of the Sailors I had served with on USS

Nevada was now the head pastor at a church in Post Falls, Idaho. When we served together, he had come to the Lord through a seed I planted. I got his number and gave him a call. It was great to catch up on what the Lord had done for him and how his ministry was growing. It was right after I talked to him that the Lord revealed to me he was the Love pastor. So, Pastor Drew Foster would be associated with the Love cabin. This left Joy to be named and I sensed in my spirit that the Lord would have me meet the Joy pastor upon our return to the states.

The other thing the Lord showed me was that right next to Faith would be a fellowship building where we would serve breakfast and have our fellowship time with the pastors that came to Briar Creek Retreat Center. He wanted this building to be called Grace.

One of the first things Gretchen and I did after getting the vision was to find out where Theodosia, Missouri was. We found it was a little town near the Arkansas state line in South Central Missouri in Ozark County. We subscribed to the Ozark County Times newspaper and had it delivered to Guam. Over time, as we poured over it each week, we got to know the issues facing the people there and really just fell in love with the place before we had ever had a chance to visit.

I felt prompted to send a letter to one of the reporters at the newspaper. Addressing the letter to Mrs. Sue Ann Jones and after giving her some of my background and how faith had worked in my life, I explained:

"About a year ago, I started thinking about the name Theodosia, and why the Lord wanted that to be His place for the Retreat Center. I knew that "Theo" meant God in Latin, but was curious to find out what the "dosia" part meant. I was shocked upon finding the word meant "God's Gift".

This now leads me to my next step. It just so happens that right after my vision was given to me, my father called to tell me he was moving to Arkansas. I told him I would be moving to Missouri and we would only be a few hours away. "Praise God, what a blessing" I thought. My family will be flying from Seattle to Little Rock this Thanksgiving so I can spend it with my father and the rest of my family. During Friday and Saturday after Thanksgiving, my wife and I will be coming to Theodosia for the first time. I don't know what to expect, but if the Lord is willing, He will show me what to look for. You can't imagine my excitement to see "God's Gift."

Sue Ann, this letter may be used however you feel led, or may only be read by you; however, in the future you will have proof that the Lord revealed this vision before my family ever arrived. Maybe with your knowledge of the area, you might shed some light on why the Lord has named it Briar Creek. Or maybe you know a realtor who can show me some property the weekend after Thanksgiving. I now leave that up to you."

She wrote me back and said she would keep a copy of my letter for future reference. She didn't know of a Briar Creek but she wouldn't be surprised if there was one, since there are thousands of little creeks all over the Ozarks. She then gave me the name of a realtor in Theodosia that she recommended.

The next thing that happened that summer blew us away. For the sake of keeping their names anonymous, a friend of mine came up to me and asked when I would be going to Missouri. I told him we planned to go up there at Thanksgiving. He said, "That should give me enough time." I said, "For what?" He said, "We want to give you and Gretchen the down payment on the land." I was literally stunned and didn't know what to say.

Gretchen and I were always the ones that gave surprises to other people, and now it was coming to us. I felt very humbled and empowered at the same time.

I got in touch with Doreen, the realtor in Theodosia, and told her I was looking for some property. After telling her what I thought would be the price range, also said the 10-12 acre range would work for what the Lord had shown me. She started emailing me different properties she currently had in Theodosia. She also agreed to devote the Friday and Saturday after Thanksgiving to Gretchen and me.

On September 1, 2007, we flew back to Washington State and moved into our new house. We got the kids in school and planned for our Thanksgiving trip and our first visit to Theodosia.

Chapter 16 - Theodosia

The time finally came and we flew out to Arkansas to spend Thanksgiving with my dad. On Friday, November 23, 2007, Gretchen and I drove up to Theodosia, Missouri, for the first time. At this point we had been getting the Ozark County Times for three years and when we first drove into town as we recognized a business, church, or school, we got all excited to finally see where everything was.

God sure works in mysterious ways because a week or so before our trip to Theodosia, the Lord made a request of me. He instructed me to make a note on a slip of paper and on the day we arrived at Theodosia, go to a grocery store in town, go in, pay for the groceries of the person at the counter, and give them this note:

"Hello,

The reason you are receiving this card is you have just been blessed with free groceries. I don't know if you are male or female. I don't know if you have a family or live by yourself. I don't know if you are rich or in need. All I know is that the Lord has impressed upon me to come to this place of Theodosia, Missouri, to this grocery store and pay for your groceries. I don't know if you are a

believer in Jesus or not; I hope if you
aren't you would consider it. I know
He loves you and His sending me to
you at this time is proof that He has
you on His mind. I pray for God's
blessing on you."

At first I was kind of confused as to why
the Lord would have me do this project on the very
day that we would be looking at land. Deep down
inside I thought it might keep me from getting
prideful about buying this land. All day, as we
looked at the different properties, I had this future
delivery in the back of my mind.

We arrived at Doreen's office and she had
invited Don, another realtor, to show us his
properties first, so that we would be able to see
everything during our visit. We jumped in Don's
truck and went to the first property. Now the
normal questions a realtor would expect to answer
would be, "Is there power available?" or "How
deep do wells usually have to be drilled?" That
wasn't what was on my mind. I simply asked him
if the property was in Theodosia. He told me it
was actually in Thornfield, but it was closer to
Theodosia than Thornfield. I told him it just
wouldn't do. We went to the next property and
again, even though the property was a beautiful
piece of land, I asked him the same question. He
said it was not in Theodosia, and "I guess that's not

going to work for you." When I finally get to move there, I hope to explain to him why it had to be Theodosia. We needed to do everything exactly how the Lord had instructed.

We dropped off Don and got into Doreen's car. I don't remember how many properties we looked at, but remember coming to the realization that 10-12 acres was just not big enough for what the Lord has shown me...especially with the trail. She had one piece of land that was 26.5 acres but it was not in my original price range. When I looked at the MLS (Multiple Listing Service) number on the packet, it was my birth date. I thought that was very curious.

Doreen explained that one side of the property was a county road, but we wouldn't be able to walk into the property from the road because there were too many briars growing there. Hmmm....briars; that's interesting. She said we could walk around the corner along the neighbor's fence and crawl onto the property from there. We pulled up and, sure enough, the area around the road was covered in briars. We walked onto the property from the neighbor's fence and walked down a gentle slope.

There was a main creek that ran the length of the property and it was named the Little Cedar Creek. However, before we got to the main creek, I saw that we had stepped over two other creeks that ran into the Little Cedar. I asked Doreen if they had names and she didn't think so. I turned around to Gretchen and said, "Maybe we'll just have to name this one Briar Creek." Doreen turned around and said, "Well, this is Briar Hollow." Just then the Lord said to me, "I brought you to a place where there are briars and creeks." I knew this was the place but I kept it to myself.

After traipsing around the property and discovering that the Little Cedar Creek had a beautiful waterfall, we went back to Doreen's office. I went into the restroom and Gretchen told Doreen that we probably wouldn't know for a few days. She explained that I always prayed about something for at least two-to-three days before making a decision. When I went into the restroom, I said a very short prayer that was basically, "Well, Lord, what do you think?" He said very clearly, "It is time to plant the mustard seed."

I came out and shocked both women by saying we'd take it. Now we needed to buy someone's groceries before the store closed.

We signed the paperwork and got across the street to the only grocery store in town. I was so excited to be able to do this after such an awesome day of finding Briar Creek. I walked into the store and the only people there were the workers. I thought I would hang out for a little while to see if someone came in, but even after picking up some water, no one came in. I paid for my water and while walking across the parking lot said, "Lord, did I miss something again?" And as He reminded me of the time back in Port Townsend, He said, "No, I was just checking your obedience." I almost cried right there. What a joyful day He gave us.

Chapter 17 - Love and Joy

Finally I was able to get to Post Falls, Idaho, and see my friend, Pastor Drew (the Love Pastor). We served together on the USS Nevada and during one underway, he came to a recommitment to Christ. Over the next few years I watched him mature in the Lord and eventually he got out of the Navy and got ordained. Even though we lost touch for a number of years, I finally had the chance to visit him at his church. To see someone making such an impact for the Kingdom in whom I had planted seeds early on was a great experience.

One Saturday night we were together in Pastor Drew's office as he was preparing for his Sunday service. I asked him, "Drew, why do you think the Lord called you the Love Pastor?" He said, "Let me show you something." He pulled out a binder and showed me the first sermon he ever gave. It was on Love. He then explained that this same sermon was the one he gave to get the job at his new church. The next morning I was able to meet the church body and there was a deep sense of love present. They seemed to genuinely care for each other and desired to reach out to their neighbors. I could see that Pleasant View had a real Love ministry.

The Joy Pastor was not as clear. Up to the time of leaving Guam, Joy was not defined. I did sense that the pastor I would meet when returning to the states would be the Joy Pastor.

Our family was invited by our long time friend, Belinda, to go to Hillcrest Assembly of God in East Bremerton, Washington. I enjoyed being back in the Assemblies of God because I liked their worship and they had an incredible children's pastor. We joined an adult Sunday school group led by Abe and Kay Young and Gretchen and I really enjoyed their teaching. To make it even better, Abe and Kay had a Wednesday night home fellowship that we also started attending. Abe got me involved right away and I quickly adopted him as my spiritual mentor.

For that season, I started experiencing joy in my own life and so I assumed that Pastor Scott Fontenot to be the Joy Pastor. I revealed it to him one day and he told me it made sense to him. He said that it was a real joy to be able to be the pastor of Hillcrest because he had wanted it for such a long time.

What seemed to be going well with me was not the case for my son Michael. He wanted to be involved but there just seemed to be something preventing it. We were invited to visit a little church up in Port Gamble, Washington, called New Covenant Fellowship. The first day we came Michael was offered a job as the sound technician in the balcony.

Every single person seemed to embrace us right off the bat.

It was here that I realized every Pastor I would ever meet from this time forward would be my Joy Pastor. The joy that I had tried to place on one pastor was actually turning into a gift of the Spirit that I would experience with every pastor I met. Pastors had become my Joy.

It was at New Covenant Fellowship that I met Pastor Bob Smith. Pastor Bob had been through the wringer. He had put up with more than any Pastor I had ever known and what emerged was a confident yet humble man. He allowed me to preach (or teach) during Sunday services and these were great growing experiences. It was also at New Covenant that I met my best friend and his wife, Danny and Suzy Claflin. As our family is now getting ready to make our move to Missouri, we will miss them more than I could ever describe.

Chapter 18 - Summer 2008

Six months had passed since we closed on the property and I was itching to get back to Theodosia. I took different mapping and survey sources off the internet and created a topographical map of the property. I used this map to measure the location where the entrance to Briar Creek would start and the location of cabin Faith. If the driveway was going to be at the center of the property, I calculated the driveway needed to be 555 feet from the end of each property line on the county road. My intention for going out to Briar Creek was to install a driveway to the Faith building site, get a well drilled and put up a sign saying, "Future Home of Briar Creek Retreat Center."

We had the sign made and rented a cabin about a mile from the property. Everything seemed to be coming together for the summer trip and we stood on faith that God would provide the resources we needed. Requiring even more faith was the fact that the gas prices started creeping up as the summer got closer. It was during the month of May the price of gas went past $4.00 a gallon and my measure of faith started to falter. More and more, it didn't look like we were going to have enough money to go out to Missouri and get anything done.

At that same time, during one of our Sunday morning services at Hillcrest Assembly, there was a visiting missionary from Mexico. He gave a small presentation and one of the things he said was, "Faith is like those doors at Wal-Mart. As you walk to the doors, you know that as soon as you get close enough the doors are going to open, so you just have to keep walking." I took that lesson to heart and continued making plans for going.

It wasn't a day or two later that my friend, who previously had generously helped us get the property, contacted me and said he was ready to wire me more money for our trip. God had once again come through for us just when it was needed.

Prior to leaving on the trip, I had been in prayer regarding the location of the well to be drilled. I had imagined, using my home-made map, that the area to the north of the Faith building site made a lot of sense for the placement of the well. Mostly this was because of where the power poles were located on the main road. During a time of worship, the Lord gave me a picture in my mind of an oak tree that marked where He wanted me to place the well, but I had to find that tree when I got there.

The time finally came and we loaded up the truck with the sign and other gear I would need to work on the land. Five days later, we arrived back in Theodosia. We checked into our cabin and after dropping off Gretchen and our supplies, I took the boys and we drove out to Briar Creek. The boys had not been on our other visit to the property so this was their first chance to see it. As I rounded the last turn and saw the property on the left, we noticed a group of half a dozen rabbits sitting in the road. I said a quick prayer, "Lord, it would sure be nice if you could have those rabbits jump into the briars where you want the driveway." Then, just as I had said the prayer, the rabbits all jumped into the property and I parked the truck at that spot.

I got out my measuring wheel and walked over to the southern-most property line. Using my wheel, I walked back 555 feet. The spot I had originally planned was right where the truck was sitting, right where the rabbits had jumped in. Just then, Michael noticed that across the road was a marker that had two flat rocks stacked in a way to make a pyramid shape. He asked me what I thought the rocks were marking. It couldn't have been a property line marker because fences were erected to show the property lines and they were no where near any boundaries. I took it as a third confirmation of the location to Briar Creek's future driveway.

Doreen, our realtor, recommended an excavator by the name of Steve Hart. I got hold of Steve prior to driving out to Missouri and arranged to meet with him the morning after our arrival. He met with me and I shared the vision of Briar Creek with him. We discussed putting in the driveway and 300 feet of rock. He said he'd bring out his bulldozer and we agreed to start the next morning at 6:30 am. That afternoon, I tried to make a path through the briars so that Gretchen and the boys could access the property a little easier. As I made it through the briars and brush, I took my orange marking spray paint and made dashed lines so that I could find it again later.

At 6:30 the next morning, I got to the property and Steve already had the bulldozer at the Faith building site. He stopped the bulldozer and I asked him how he knew where to go. He just said he followed my dashed line. Praise God! His guiding hand had even directed Steve.

By 8:00 a.m. Steve was almost done and asked me if the wife and kids were going to come by. I told him they all planned to go into Branson to the Silver Dollar City amusement park. Steve said he would probably be done by then, if I wanted to go with them. I told him I didn't really want to go, and he replied, "I'll take my time."

A few hours later, we had a 300 foot driveway put in, three truckloads of rock were poured, and four holes were drilled for the sign and driveway posts. Now I had to find the oak tree where the well was going to be. Until I could find the tree, I couldn't have a driller come out to give me a bid. On the day before I had to start driving back to Washington, I had parked the truck looking up the drive instead of parking down toward the creek. Looking to my right, there was the tree. I hadn't noticed it until the bulldozer had cleared the trees around it and I had to be facing east in order to see it at the angle the Lord had shown me. I was happy to know where the well would go, but also realized the Lord wanted me to have the well drilled at a later date because there just wasn't enough time to do it on this trip.

It was only after we got back home to Washington I realized something about the place of the well. While looking at the property with Google Earth™ and marking the well location on my map, I saw that the creek we had walked over on our first visit and I had said to Gretchen, "Maybe we'll just have to call this Briar Creek," started where the oak tree stood. It is possible that Briar Creek is being fed by a spring and that is where the Lord directed the well. I will find that out when I get back there.

Chapter 19 - Hope

It is now approaching the summer of 2010. It has been two years since we were at the property. It has not been easy to wait on the Lord to do His next step. Originally I envisioned this chapter would be named Patience because that is what has been tested in me these last two years. Instead it is named Hope. Only recently have I realized that I have been living in a constant state of Hope.

In order to understand Hope, we should first look at what Hope is not. Hope is not "wishful thinking" as most people would say it is. Hope comes from the Greek word 'elpis' which means "confident expectation" or "anticipation." Hope becomes the expectation of a reality we don't see. Faith, too, is "the substance of things hoped for, the evidence of things not seen" (Hebrews 11:1).

This isn't the definition of Faith; instead, the word substance takes on the meaning of "reality." What Faith has done is taken the things hoped for and treated them as reality. This reality then becomes the proof that what is unseen is actually real. Hope and Faith are intertwined. I approach Briar Creek in the same way. I believe what is hoped for already exists. Going into something believing it is already a reality might seem like a fallacy, but this is what Faith is all about. Having Hope takes believing and trusts in a God who is always reliable and who always has my best interest at heart.

I came to the point of trusting the Lord for every step. This vision is way too big for me. There is no way I can ever earn enough money in my lifetime to build and run this retreat, at least to the extent the Lord has shown me. But, when I take the Faith of God's vision of Briar Creek and I add Hope, I am able to wait for His next word.

My time in the Navy has finally come to a close. On June 16, 2010, I will retire. Two days later Michael will graduate from High School. On June 24, Michael flies to Belize, Central America, for a five-month mission trip and the rest of us move to Missouri.

We go on Faith as we Hope in the Lord. Just like Abraham was told to move to a place he didn't know, we go to a place we don't know. We do, however, look forward to living in Theodosia, "God's Gift."

I pray that as each shovel goes into the ground and as each nail is hammered into wood at Briar Creek, this work will be done with Love. Scriptures tell us to abide in Faith, Hope, and Love, but the greatest of these is Love (1 Corinthians 13:13). Faith will enable us by making Hope a reality, and as the unseen become real, we must remember to push toward Love. It will only be through Love that we can learn to imitate our Lord and King, Jesus Christ. Amen.

If you are interested in the ministry at Briar Creek,
send me an email at:
briarcreekretreat@gmail.com

Made in the USA
Las Vegas, NV
28 May 2021